FANFARE

JON GEORGE

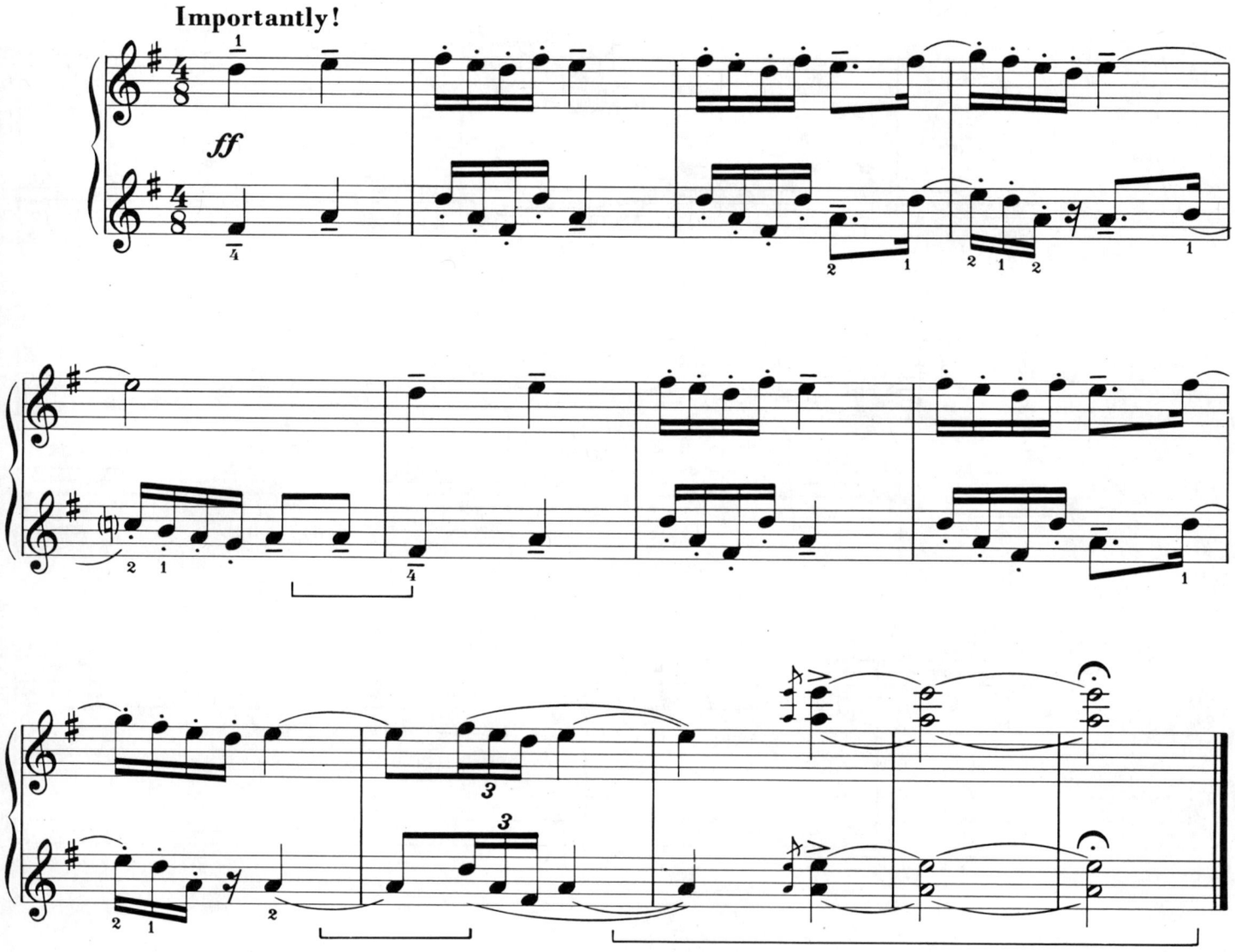

© Oxford University Press, Inc. 1972. Assigned to Oxford University Press 2010. Printed in the U.S.A.

PROCESSIONAL

MEDIAEVAL PAGEANT

CONTENTS

FANFARE, 3
PROCESSIONAL, 4
THE TOURNAMENT BEGINS, 5
THE TROUBADOUR SINGS, 7
THE JESTER PERFORMS, 8
MINIATURE SUITE, 10
1. BRANLE, 10
2. AIR, 12
3. GIGGE, 14

ILLUSTRATIONS AND DESIGN BY DIANNE WEISS

JON GEORGE

MEDIAEVAL PAGEANT

EASY PIANO PIECES FOR THE YOUNG PERFORMER

OXFORD UNIVERSITY PRESS

THE TOURNAMENT BEGINS

f
Everyone is anxiously awaiting the first event.
f
ff

THE TROUBADOUR SINGS

THE JESTER PERFORMS

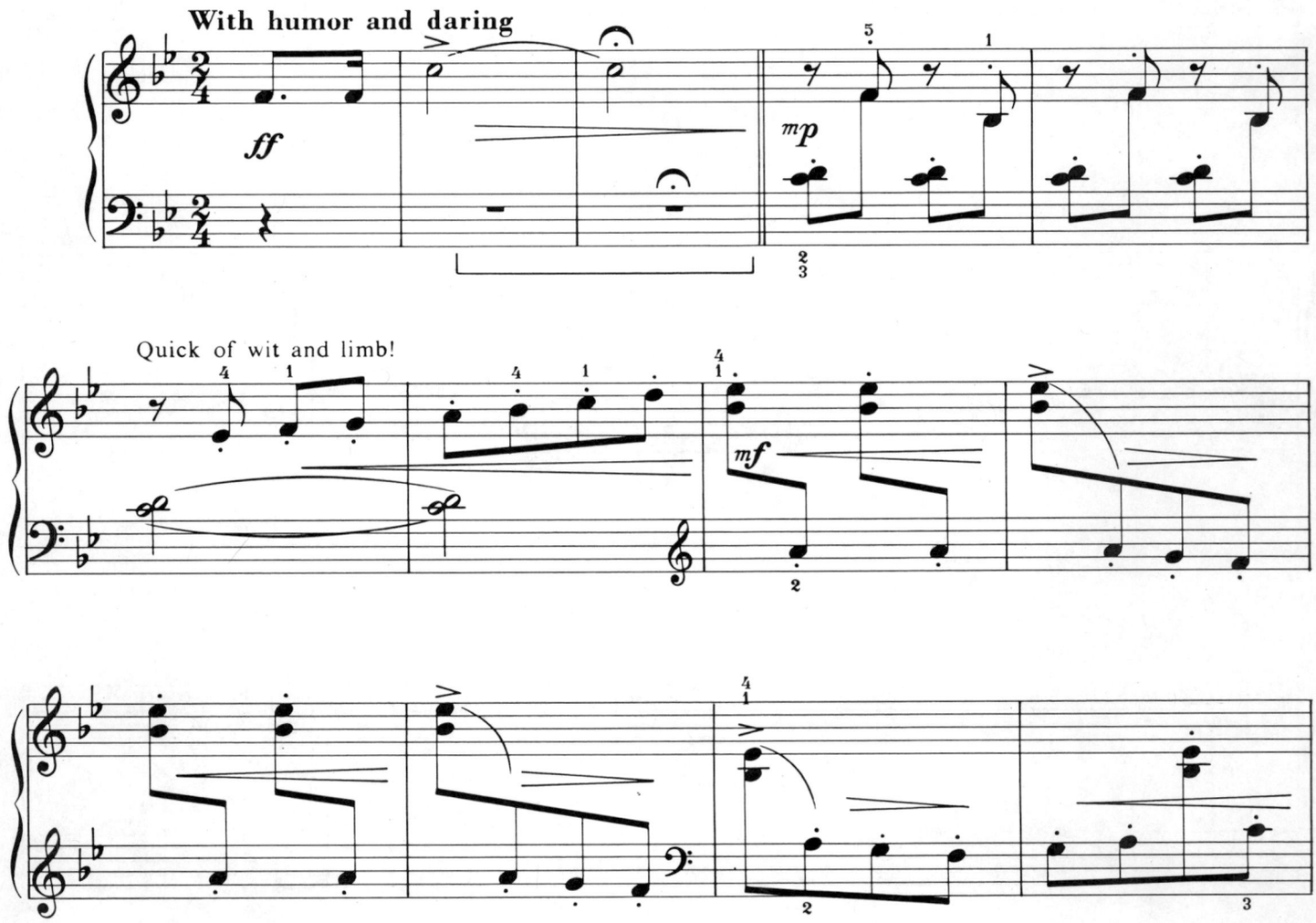

p
mf
p
f
He has the king roaring with laughter!
mp subito
mf
8va
Look! he even does cartwheels!
f
p

MINIATURE SUITE

1. BRANLE

5
mf a tempo
5
2
2

2. AIR

rit.

3. GIGGE

mp
f
mp
sfz

ISBN 978-0-19-385488-
9 780193 854888